AMAZING
DOGS
COLORING BOOK

FOR CHILDREN

BRIGHT GODSON C.

ELEMENTARY TEACHER

HELLO KIDS,

THIS COLORING BOOK HAS BEEN DESIGNED SPECIALLY FOR YOU, TO COLOR YOUR FAVORITE DOGS. WE HAVE SELECTED FORTY FOUR FA-VORITE DOGS THAT YOU WILL DEFINITELY LOVE.

GRAB YOUR COLORS AND PAINT THE DOGS TO BECOME YOUR FAVORITE CUTE DOGS!!

BABY
PINKY
LIKES TO
SPIT!

JACKSON
IS HUNGRY
WHAT WILL
HE EAT?

THIS IS CUTE

OLIVIA,

SHE IS A

LOVELY PUPPY

I
LOVE
TO
PLAY

ANCHOR
IS A
LOVELY
PUPPY

PAUL AND PETER STANDING NEAR A FENCE. THEY LOVE STANDING THERE. THEY ARE ALWAYS HAPPY. THEY STAND THERE TO DISCUSS BONES THEY STOLE AND LAUGH AT SCHOOL CHIDREN WALKING TO SCHOOL.

TWO CUTE PUPPIES

MR BONE
IS A BRAVE DOG.
HE LIKES TO SIT ALONE.

HE HAS RESCUED
HIS OWNER'S BABY
FORM DROWNING
IN A NEARBY STREAM

ANCHOR
IS A
LOVELY
PUPPY

CAN YOU GUESS
WHAT HE IS
THINKING...???

GRAND UNCLE SAM
LOVES STAYING ALONE.
HE IS ALWAYS THINKING
OF HIS OLD AGE

PUPPY
WINKS
THE EYE

MOTHER DOG
LOVES
STICKING
OUT HER
TONGUE

JACK

THIS IS BUDDY
HE IS A GRAND DOG
HE LOVES STAYING ALONE

DO YOU KNOW WHAT I AM THINKING?

YAY!!

CAN YOU
SMILE

LIKE ME?

THE SHEPARD

CHAINED DOG WANTS
TO JUMP

I HAVE A BIG
HEAD

MOTHER AND DAUGHTER SMILING

BABY ANDRES
LOVES TO
SMILE